SUNNY SIDE UP!

Published by
The Curtis Publishing Company
Indianapolis, Indiana

Sunny Side Up
is dedicated to my daughters,
Jana and Jennifer,
who brighten up my day.

SUNNY SIDE UP

Printed in the United States of America.

For information address
The Curtis Publishing Company
1100 Waterway Boulevard
Indianapolis, Indiana 46202

Library Congress Catalog Card Number 83-062754
ISBN 0-89387-075-7

"Here's your sunny-side-ups, sir!"

"When do I get to go to lunch? How come this chair is so hard? It's drafty in here. I don't like my hours. When do I . . ."

"Matter-of-fact,
I *do* have a picture of my ex-wife on me."

"Just be patient—in a few more minutes
he'll throw *all* his bait away."

"What's wrong with your *gyne*, mom?"

"If I were a woman,
I'd smack your face for saying that!"

"Well, God has to sleep sometime, too!"

"No, we can't pretend you took your bath!"

"Why don't you pick on somebody your *own* size?"

"I would never say anything like that!"

"I don't feel like racing anymore!"

"Now where did I plant those forget-me-nots?"

"I need some *water pills!*"

"Would you like a little batter with your fish?"

"You bellyached?"

"Get out of the sun,
Rudy, you're starting to melt!"

"I don't care who you are or where you're from,
you've just ruined my lawn!"

"I must have slept on my neck wrong last night!"

BRAIN STORM

"I wish Jacques Cousteau would mind his own business!"

" . . . An emergency landing?
But, captain, didn't you see that sign?"

"Personally, I'd prefer a shower!"

"Raymond, I'm sorry to see
your allergy is bothering you again!"

"I wonder why they go to all that trouble
to get a temporary job?"

"Dad, do fish pee?"

"For the last time, no! You can't keep that stupid dog.
By the way, where is he?"

"I want you to quit feeding your face
and clean up your room!"

"This way I can brag to all the guys at the office
that I run around like they do."

"I don't know what it is,
but you'd better not play with it."

"I don't care what they're paying Pete Rose,
your allowance is staying the same."

"I want to be a *cop* when I grow up!"

"I don't want a square meal, grandma.
The corners might hurt my tummy!"

"This is supposed to be a vacation!"

PUSHING A BROOM

"The last three years I've gone around the world.
This year, I'd like to go somewhere else."

''Can you hear me now?''

"This is the place I was telling you about."

"I can *so* arrest you in a safety zone!"

"Male chauvinist *piggy*!"

"You idiot, who's going to believe
a little birdie told me that!"

"Mommy, does this chicken know we're eating him?"

"Here comes lunch."

" . . . But this little piggy
doesn't want to go to market!"

"Honest, I hate fried chicken . . ."

"Did you call for a cab?"

"You're going to have to stop petting your porcupine."

"Mom, I'm sure glad you named me Johnnie,
cause that's what all my friends call me!"

"Could I have a glass of water, please?"

"We have a temporary loss of picture . . . . *we continue with the sound . . . with the sound . . . with the sound . . . with the sound . . .*

"I'm sorry, Mr. Farwick, but your wife
is turning into a vegetable!"

"Have you ever had legionaire's disease?"

"I'm not going to *wear my hair*
for you anymore, Sheldon!"

"Sarge, someone ripped-off
our *crime prevention week* buttons!"

"All I got was two *horrible* mentions!"

"You kids stop that!
You're going to upset mommie's mood ring!"

"Darling, I just love the new jumpsuit you got me!"

"Pass the ketchup!"

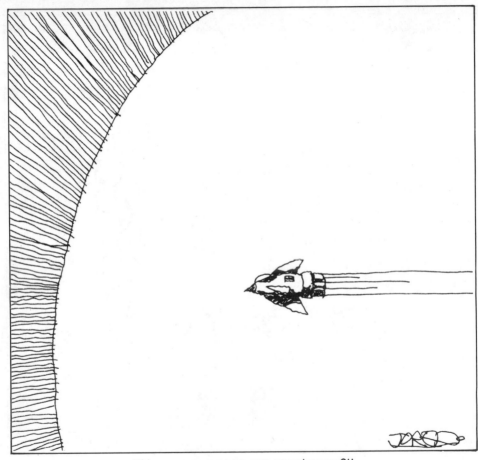

"Has anyone seen my sunglasses?"